THE SAYINGS OF MUHAMMAD.

EDITED BY

ABDULLAH AL-MĀMŪN AL-SUHRAWARDY.
M. A., M. R. A. S.

يُرِيدُونَ لِيُطْفِئُوا نُورَ اللَّهِ بِأَفْوَاهِهِمْ

وَاللَّهُ مُتِمُّ نُورِهِ وَلَوْ كَرِهَ الْكَافِرُونَ ۝

They desire to put out the **Light of God** *with their mouths; but God will perfect His light, averse though the faithless people be! — Kur'ān.*

LONDON
ARCHIBALD CONSTABLE & Co. Ltd
16 James Street. Haymarket.
1905.

Printed by E. J. BRILL, Leyden (Holland).

TO MY MOTHER.

الجَنَّةُ تَحْتَ اَقْدَامِ الأُمَّهَاتِ

Heaven lieth at the feet of mothers. — MUHAMMAD. صلعم

لَقَدْ كَانَ لَكُمْ فِي رَسُوْلِ اللّٰهِ أُسْوَةٌ حَسَنَةٌ ۞

An excellent pattern had ye in the Messenger of God. — Kur'ān.

FOREWORD.

The supreme importance of the sayings of Muhammad, apart from their general ethical value, can be fully realised only when one becomes aware that the whole religious, moral, social and political fabric of a vast section of humanity rests on the Book (the Kur'ān), the sayings and acts (the Sunnah) of the Prophet, and analogical deductions therefrom.

The Ways and Wont of Muhammad and his utterances form a living commentary on and a supplement to the Kur'ān. Their great importance and their difference from the *obiter dicta* of other teachers lie in this: the utterances of other prophets, sages, and philosophers may become the object of enthusiastic admiration in the absence of any sanction to enforce their translation into practice; whereas the utterances of Muhammad have already acquired the force of law. A Muslim may question the genuineness of an individual saying; but once its authenticity is proved it is as binding upon him as the injunctions and prohibitions in the Kur'ān. What a powerful influence the example of the Prophet exercises over the hearts and imaginations of his followers may well be realised from the fact that to-day the approved mode of parting the hair and of wearing the beard, and the popularity of the turban and flowing robes in the East, are all due to the conscious or unconscious imitation of that great Leader of Fashion who flourished in Arabia at the beginning of the seventh century. Nor is this 'Imitation' of Muhammad confined to that of his 'animal actions'.

Nobler minds always strive after the Ideal. The chance words that fell from the lips of that marvellous and gifted Teacher during the twenty years of his ministry were treasured up by his eager listeners and embalmed in their hearts, and became the ruling principles of their actions. Islām has had its martyrs, its saints, its recluses, and ascetics who have illustrated in their lives the true significance of their Faith — self-surrender, self-abnegation, Verneinung des Willens. But, alas, (be it said to the discredit of his head if not to that of his heart), the Muslim, blinded by his deep reverence for the Prophet, attaches equal importance to all his sayings and acts, and refuses to distinguish the permanent from the temporary and thus does a great injustice to his Master. Ibn Ḥanbal, for example, would not even eat water-melons because, although he knew the Prophet ate them, he could not learn whether he ate them with or without the rind, or whether he broke, bit, or cut them.

The Table-Talk of the Prophet deals with the most minute and delicate circumstances of life, and the collected body of the Ways and Wont of Muhammad is the Muslim's dictionary of morals and manners. It is therefore not to be wondered at that there are no less than

1,465 collections of the Prophet's sayings extant, of which the more generally used amongst the Sunnis are the 'Six Correct' collections, and those amongst the Shiahs, 'the Four Books'.

This small collection of the authentic utterances of the Prophet cannot claim to be a fair sample of the whole. It is not an index to the mind of MUHAMMAD. It is an index to the mind of Muhammad. And the mind of the Master should not be measured by that of his humble disciple.

Perhaps one will miss in this collection the hyperbolical teachings of other Masters, but the ethical sweetness, beauty, strong common sense, practicality, and modernity of thought of some of the utterances will not fail to appeal to higher minds and also strike the attention of lower natures. Some of the sayings are chosen to illustrate the rude and barbarous manners of the people amongst whom the Law-giver lived, whilst a few are specially meant for the Muslim, the mystic, the spiritualist, and the ṣūfī. If this booklet serves in the least degree to quicken the march of the spirit of Renaissance and Reform now abroad in the Dār-al-Islām, and to awaken an interest in the Faith amongst those Seekers after Truth in the West who are worshippers of the Light and not of the Lamp, the labours of the compiler will be more than amply rewarded.

MUHAMMAD.

محمد الداعی

The Pan-Islamic Society,
LONDON, *February* 1905.

I.

MUHAMMAD.

> *And the life of Muhammad is not the life of a God, but of a man; from first to last it is intensely human.* — Lane-Poole.

From more than one point of view, the system established by the great Arabian reformer Muhammad is worthy of serious study. That one of the leading Christian Powers should also be the greatest Muslim Power of modern times is a striking fact, testifying to a degree of toleration which would have been impossible to the Christianity of the Middle Ages, and also showing that even for prudential considerations it is well for Englishmen to understand a religion with which they are brought into close relationship. Moreover, the religion of Muhammad is the only serious rival to Christianity; and, being from the simplicity of its main conception and the suitability of its ordinances well adapted to the needs of the races of the East, it has, especially in Africa, advanced with a rapidity which Christian missionaries are unable either to check or to emulate.

A brief sketch of Muhammad's life will form a suitable introduction to an account of his religious system. Most faiths centre in a great personality, and this is specially true of Islām. There are no "historic doubts" as to the actual existence of Muhammad; throughout his active career almost every detail of his life is known. That career is of extraordinary interest; that character was one of the most powerful influences in human history.

Arabia, about the time of Muhammad's birth, at Mecca, in A.D. 570, was in a state of religious unrest and political chaos. Its wandering inhabitants, who are believed to have been descendants of Abraham through Ishmael, and therefore closely akin to the Jewish people, were mainly idolaters, worshipping stars, stones, and fetishes. There were many Jewish colonies which had been established after the destruction of Jerusalem 500 years earlier, while a number of Christian sects made the influence of their faith in more or less debased forms perceptible among the native tribes. The chief of these sects were the Nestorians, the Arians, the Sabellians, the Eutychians, the Marianites, the Collyridians; but many other forms of religious eccentricity flourished in the freedom of the desert. There were also men known as Ḥanīfs, who did not attach themselves to any religious community, but were anchorites of an individualist and ascetic character, who taught a monotheistic faith in which elements of Essenism and Christianity were mingled. This comparative purity of life and doctrine doubtless helped to prevent the utter decay of religion in the Arabian peninsula; but the urgent need of moral reform was perceived by many before the advent of Muhammad. Indeed, a widespread expectation was in the air that the time was approaching when an Arabian Messiah should appear and found a new religion. The ground was prepared for a great social and religious revolution. The time was ripe, and the man appeared.

The father of Muhammad died before his son's birth, and the boy having at six years of age lost his mother also, was brought up by his uncle, Abū Ṭālib, who, though not a believer in his mission, remained through life the Prophet's best friend. Until manhood, Muhammad was in poor circumstances, tending flocks of sheep and assisting his uncle in his business as a merchant. At the age of twenty-five, Muhammad, through the offices of Abū Ṭālib, obtained employment as a camel driver with a rich widow named Khạdījah, and took charge of a caravan conveying merchandise to Syria. Pleased with his successful management, and attracted by his personal beauty, Khadījah, though by fiften years his senior, sent her sister to offer the young man her hand in marriage. Matters were promptly arranged, and Muhammad became a man of wealth and position. No great success, however, attended his own business enterprises. Religion and commerce sometimes require a good deal of reconciling, and Muhammad was not then an adept in the art of making the best of both worlds. Naturally reserved, and with a mind disposed to a poetic and dreamy mysticism, his mundane affairs were somewhat neglected. His religion assumed an increasingly earnest tone; he spent a large part of his time in lonely meditation in the desert and among the hills, and many an unseen conflict left its trace upon his soul.

Not until he was forty years old did Muhammad receive his first "divine revelation", in the solitude of the mountains near Mecca. Translated into modern language, this means that he then first became convinced that he had a mission to fulfil, viz., to arouse men from their sins, their indifference, their superstition, to thunder into their ears a message from on high, and awaken them to living faith in one indivisible, all-powerful, and all-merciful God. Prolonged fasting, days of ecstatic contemplation, and vigils of the night in the silent valleys and gloomy mountain caves had made him a visionary, with a firm faith that God had inspired him to be His messenger to mankind. This revelation, generally believed to be referred to in the short 96th sūrah of the Kur'ān, he communicated to none but his immediate relatives and a faithful friend, Abū Bakr. Painful doubts as to the reality of the vision oppressed him, but were dispelled by the sympathy of his friends. Haunted for a long time by these doubts of the divinity of his mission, his depression became so great that he was more than once on the point of committing suicide. Many of his friends called him a fool, a liar, a mad poet; and the city of Mecca for several years illustrated the proverb that a prophet hath no honour in his own country by a decisive rejection of his claims. When conviction, however, had once taken possession of his mind, it was unshakable. When his uncle begged him to cease his attempts to convert the Meccans, and so put an end to constant trouble, Muhammad said: "Though they gave me the sun in my right hand and the moon in my left to bring me back from my undertaking, yet will I not pause till the Lord carry His cause to victory, or till I die for it." Turning away, he burst into tears, and Abū Ṭālib replied: "Go in peace, son of my brother, and say what thou wilt, for by God I will on no condition abandon thee."

The little body of believers grew slowly. In four years Muhammad had about forty proselytes, mostly of the lower ranks, and he then felt himself justified in coming forward as a public preacher and denouncing the superstitions of the Meccans. To establish a new religion was no part of his intention; he desired simply to recall them to the purer and truer faith of their ancestor, Abraham. Zealous for the worship of the Ka'bah, and dreading lest the profitable pilgrimages to their city should fall into decay, the people of Mecca showed the bitterest hostility to Muhammad, opposing and ridiculing him at every turn. So violent was their hatred that Abū Ṭālib thought it prudent to shelter him for a time in a place of security in the country. About this time his wife died, then his uncle, and changes of fortune reduced him again to poverty. He went to another part of the country, but found himself in danger, and barely escaped with his life. But a turning-point in his career was at hand. In a party of pilgrims from the rival city of Yathrib, afterwards called Medinah, Muhammad made several converts. On their visit the following year, their numbers were so greatly increased that Muhammad entered into an alliance with them, and on a certain night, when a plot had been made to assassinate him he left the city of his birth and took refuge in the friendly city. The Muslim era or Hegira (Hijrah) dates from this event.

Muhammad was now among friends; his converts increased rapidly in number and the once despised Teacher was recognised as the ruler of a city and of two powerful tribes. Missionaries were sent to all parts of Arabia, and even to neighbouring countries, including Egypt and Persia; and a year later the Prophet celebrated the pilgrimage in peace in the holy city of his enemies. The final conquest of Mecca was followed by the submission of the tribes and the acknowledgment of Muhammad's spiritual and temporal supremacy over the Arabian peninsula. The vanquished marvelled at the magnanimity of the victor. Only three or four persons, and those criminals, were put to death, and a general amnesty was then proclaimed. His strenuous labours, his intense excitement, the grief for the loss of his little boy Ibrahīm, and the excruciating pain sometimes felt from the poison administered to him by a Jewess at Khaibar, further combined to weaken his frame. He became aware that his end was approaching; he addressed his followers in the mosque as often as he was able, exhorting them to righteousness and piety and peace among themselves. Each man, he declared, must work out his own salvation. He read passages from the Kur'ān, asked forgiveness of any whom he had wronged, appointed his successors, and prepared his weeping followers for his death. His head pillowed on the lap of his wife, his lips murmuring of pardon and paradise, the dying agonies of a great soul came to an end, and the Preacher of Islām breathed his last.

His people were moved to keen distress. Omar, half-frantic, drew his scimitar, rushed among the crowd, and declared he would strike off the head of anyone who dared to say the prophet of God was no more. Abū Bakr calmed him, and preached resignation to the will of God.

Muhammad was a man of imposing

presence, of medium height, broad-shouldered, and strongly built, with fine features, coal-black hair and eyes, and a long beard. His mental powers were of a high order, his manners reserved yet affable and courteous; his speech laconic and often humorous, a man of strong passions but noble impulses, capable of great love, great generosity, altogether a character of surprising force, capacity, shrewdness, and determination. Temperate and prudent in youth, he gained in manhood the name of "al-Amīn", or "the faithful", from his fair and upright dealing. Just and affectionate in private life, he lived in the humblest style in a poor hut, eating the plainest food, lighting his own fire, and mending his own clothes and shoes, having given his slaves their freedom. For months together he would seldom eat a hearty meal, always sharing it with those whose need was greater: a number of the poor lived entirely on his generosity. The following beautiful story is worth passing on: "Sleeping one day under a palm tree, he awoke suddenly to find an enemy named Du'thūr standing over him with drawn sword. 'O, Muhammad, who is there now to save thee?' cried the man. 'God', answered Muhammad. Du'thūr dropped his sword. Muhammad seized it, and cried in turn: 'O, Du'thūr, who is there now to save thee?' 'No one', replied Du'thūr. 'Then learn from me to be merciful', said Muhammad, and handed him back the weapon. Du'thūr became one of his firmest friends [1]."

1 Summarised from Mr. Gorham's sketch in his *Ethics of the Great Religions.*

II.

ISLĀM.

The soul of Islām is its declaration of the unity of God: its heart is the inculcation of an absolute resignation to His will. — EDWIN ARNOLD.

The word Islām means absolute submission to God's will, self-surrender, self-abnegation, Nirvana, Verneinung des Willens, Excelsior, *Striving after the Ideal.*

The faith of Islām inculcates belief in:

1. (*a*) *One* God التوحيد.

(*b*) God's goodness and justice العدل.

2. The Immortality of the soul المعاد.

3. The Law of Duty العمل.

4. The Accountability for human actions in another existence. "Whoever doeth an atom-weight of good shall behold the same: whoever doeth an atom-weight of evil shall behold the same."

The Muslim believes in a chain of inspired prophets and teachers, who taught the above truths, beginning with the dawn of religious consciousness in man, the first Teacher of Islām being the First Man. With the evolution, progress, and advancement of humanity the Divine will reveals and manifests itself more clearly and distinctly. Hence each succeeding teacher is greater than his predecessor, inasmuch as he addresses a more advanced humanity. The Muslim, therefore, believes in the message of the Lord Jesus but not in his divinity or sonship. 'We are all of God, and towards Him are we progressing.' We are all the children of God and, in our upward progress towards Him, can attain to Christhood, nay, even surpass Christ. The spark of the Divine is latent in the heart of every atom.

النبوّة و الامامة او الخلافة

The obligatory duties taught by Islām are:

1. Ablution.[1] (Purity of Body).
2. Prayer.[1] (Purity of Heart).

---

1 5 times daily.

3. Charity.[1] (Brother-Help).
4. Fasting.[2] (Subjugation of the passions, self-abnegation).
5. Pilgrimage to Mecca.[3] (Equality and Brotherhood, — Emblem of the pilgrimage of life).

Islām forbids drinking and gambling, recognises no priesthood, no doctrines of original sin, Atonement, and Redemption. Each soul must work out its own salvation. Islām holds out a hope of salvation to all. The soul that worships the Almighty, but not the Son, the Light, but not the lamp, strives after the True, and acts aright shall have everlasting life.

---

1 2½ per cent payable in the 12th month after 11 months' possession.

2 One month in a year. — Only for the able-bodied.

3 Incumbent only on the rich.

It matters not whate'er ye name your-
selves —
Believing Muslims, Jews or Nazarenes
Or Ṣābians — whoe'er believe in God,
The last e'erlasting Day, and *act aright*,
Their meed is with their Lord; no fear
nor care
Shall come upon them, nor the touch
of woe.

— Kur'ān, 2. 59.

With the exception of a few words the transliteration of Arabic letters is that adopted by the Geneva. Congress of Orientalists.

GLOSSARY.

Companions. — The immediate disciples of Muhammad.

Dār-al-Islām. — The Home of Islām, Moslemdom.

Fire. — Hell.

Friends. — The 'companions'.

Garden. — Heaven.

Hijrah. — Lit. 'migration'. (1) Departure of Muhammad from Mecca. (2) The Muslim era. (3) A Muslim's leaving a country under non-Muslim rule. (4) Fleeing from sin.

Ignorance. — The 'Dark Age' of Arabian history, the period preceding the advent of Muhammad.

Imān. — Faith.

Mu'min. — Faithful, a Muslim.

Muslim. — A believer in Islām, a 'Mahometan'.

People of the Book. — Believers in a revealed moral religion, Jews, Christians, Ṣābians etc.

Rasūl. — Apostle, Messenger of God, a Man sent of God, a prophet.

Sūrah. — 'A row or series'. A term used for the 'chapters' öf the Kur'ān, of which there are 114 in number.

Word of God. — al-Kur'ān, the Koran.

BIBLIOGRAPHY.

AMEER ALI, *The Spirit of Islam.*

AMEER ALI, *The Ethics of Islam.*

ARNOLD, Sir EDWIN, *Pearls of the Faith.*

ARNOLD, T. W., *The Preaching of Islam.*

LANE-POOLE, S., *Studies in a Mosque.*

SMITH, R. BOSWORTH, *Mohammad and Mohammadanism.*

بسم الله الرحمن الرحيم ۞

IN GOD'S NAME, THE LOVING, THE KIND.

قال رسول الله صلعم:

I.

Actions will be judged according to intentions.

2.

The proof of a Muslim's sincerity is that he payeth no heed to that which is not his business.

3.

No man is a true believer unless he desireth for his brother that which he desireth for himself.

4.

That which is lawful is clear, and that which is unlawful likewise, but there are certain doubtful things between the two, from which it is well to abstain. [1]

1 According to Abū Dā'ūd only these four sayings of the Prophet are indispensable for the religious guidance of man and contain the summary of Islamic law.

5.

Be ye endued with divine qualities.

6.

He dieth not who giveth life to learning.

7.

Whoso honoureth the learned, honoureth me.

8.

Pray to God morning and evening, and employ the day in your avocations.

9.

He who neither worketh for himself, nor for others, will not receive the reward of God.

10.

Whoso is able and fit and doth not work for himself, or for others, God is not gracious to him.

11.

Those who earn an honest living are the beloved of God.

12.

God is gracious to him that earneth his living by his own labour, and not by begging.

13.

The best of alms is that which the right hand giveth, and the left hand knoweth not of.

14.

Charity that is concealed appeaseth the wrath of God.

15.

He is not of me, but a rebel at heart, who, when he speaketh, speaketh falsely; who, when he promiseth, breaketh his promises; and who, when trust is reposed in him, faileth in his trust.

16.

The Faithful (i. e. Muslims) are those who perform their trust and fail not in their word, and keep their pledge.

17.

Thus saith the Lord, "Verily those who are patient in adversity and forgive wrongs, are the doers of excellence."

18.

Humility and courtesy are acts of piety.

19.

True modesty is the source of all virtues.

20.

Modesty and chastity are parts of the Faith.

21.

The best of almsgiving is that which springeth from the heart, and is uttered by the lips to soften the wounds of the injured.

22.

They will enter the Garden of Bliss who have a true, pure and merciful heart.

23.

He who is not affectionate to God's creatures, and to his own children, God will not be affectionate to him.

24.

To every young person who honoureth the old, on account of their age, may God appoint those who shall honour him in his years..

25.

He is not of us who is not affectionate to his little ones, and doth not respect the reputation of the old; and he is not of us who doth not order that which is good, and prohibit that which is bad.

26.

He is true who protecteth his brother both present and absent.

27.

No man is true in the truest sense of the word but he who is true in word, in deed, and in thought.

28.

To gladden the heart of the weary, to remove the suffering of the afflicted, hath its own reward. In the day of trouble, the memory of the action cometh like a rush of the torrent, and taketh our burden away.

29.

Be persistent in good actions.

30.

He who helpeth his fellow-creature in the hour of need, and he who helpeth the oppressed him will God help in the Day of Travail.

31.

What actions are most excellent? To gladden the heart of a human being, to feed the hungry, to help the afflicted, to lighten the sorrow of the sorrowful, and to remove the wrongs of the injured.

32.

Who is the most favoured of God? He from whom the greatest good cometh to His creatures.

33.

He who trieth to remove the want of his brother, whether he be successful or not, God will forgive his sins.

34.

The best of men is he from whom good accrueth to humanity.

35.

All God's creatures are His family; and he is the most beloved of God who trieth to do most good to God's creatures.

36.

Strive always to excel in virtue and truth.

37.

Whoever is kind to His creatures, God is kind to him; therefore be kind to man on earth, whether good or bad; and being kind to the bad, is to withhold him from badness, so that those who are in Heaven may be kind to you.

38.

The people for the Abode of Bliss are three; the first, a just king, a doer of good to his people, endowed with virtue; the second, an affectionate man, of a tender heart to relations and others; the third, a virtuous man.

39.

I have left two things among you, and you will not stray as long as you hold them fast; one is the Book of God, the other the Laws of His Messenger.

40.

God hath made a straight road, with two walls, one on each side of it, in which are open doors, with curtains drawn across. At the top of the road is an Admonisher, who saith, "Go straight on the road, and not crooked;" and above this Admonisher is another who saith to any one who would pass through these doorways, "Pass not through those doors, or verily ye will fall." Now, the road is Islām; and the open doors are those things which God hath forbidden;

and the curtains before the doors the bounds set by God; the Admonisher is the Kur'ān, and the upper Admonisher *God, in the heart of every Mu'min.*

41.

My words are not contrary to the word of God, but the word of God can contradict mine, and some of the words of God abrogate others (Jābir). Muhammad said, "Some of my words rescind others, like the Kur'ān" (Ibn Omar).

42.

Verily ye are ordered the divine commandments, then forsake them not; ye are forbidden the unlawful, then do not fall therein; there are fixed boundaries, then pass not beyond them; and there is silence on some things without their being forgotten, then do not debate about them.

43.

Learn to know thyself, O 'Alī.

44.

To the light have I attained and in the light I live.

45.

My words are Law, my example is Doctrine, and my state is Truth.

46.

A perfect Muslim is he from whose tongue and hands mankind is safe, and a Muhājir [1] is he who fleeth what God hath forbidden.

47.

Inform me in the matter of Islām, so that I may have no occasion to ask others about it. Lord Muhammad said, "Say, O Sufyān, 'I believe in God;' after which obey the commandments, and abandon the things forbidden."

---

1 Those companions of the Prophet who *fled* from Mecca and went into exile with him were called Muhājirs — Performers of the Hijrah (p. xxi).

48.

If envy were proper, two persons would be the most proper objects of it; one, a man to whom God hath given riches, and appointed to bestow in charity; the other, to whom God hath granted the knowledge of religion, and who acteth thereon himself, instructing others.

49.

Men differ like mines of gold and silver, the good in Ignorance are the good in Islām, when they have obtained the knowledge of religion.

50.

That person who relieveth a Mu'min from distress in this world, God will in the like manner relieve him in the next; and he who shall do good to the indigent, God will do good to him in this world and the next.

51.

The Messenger of God was asked,

"What is the greatest vice of man?" He said, "You must not ask me about vice, but ask about virtue;" and he repeated this three times, after which he said, "Know ye! The worst of men is a bad learned man, and a good learned man is the best."

52.

Prayers lighten the heart, and charity is a proof of Imān (Faith), and abstinence from sin is perfect splendour; the Kur'ān is a proof of gain to you, if you do good, and it is a detriment to you if you do wrong;[1] and every man who riseth in the morning either doeth that which will be the means of his redemption or his ruin.

53.

Then the child (of Zainab) was brought to Lord Muhammad, dying;

---

1 Because it promises Happiness to the good and Misery to the wicked.

its soul trembling and moving; and both the eyes of the Apostle of God shed many tears. And S'ad said, "O Messenger of God! What is this weeping and shedding of tears?" [1] He said, "This is an expression of the tenderness and compassion, which the Lord hath put into the hearts of His servants; the Lord doth not compassionate and commisserate His servants, except such as are tender and full of feeling.

54.

The Apostle of God wept over S'ad b. 'Ubādah. And he said, "Have not you heard that the Lord doth not punish on account of shedding tears, nor for sobs from the hearts of the afflicted?" He is not of the people of our way who slappeth his cheeks and teareth his collar, and mourneth like the mournings of Ignorance. [2]

---

1 The disciples expected the Messenger of God to be above smiles and tears.

2 The Prophet had forbidden 'the mourn-

55.

Wish not for death, any one of you; neither the doer of good works, for peradventure he may increase them by an increase of life; nor the offender, for perhaps he may obtain the forgiveness of God by repentance. Wish not, nor supplicate for death before its time cometh; for verily when you die, hope is out and the ambition for reward; and verily, the increase of a Mu'min's life increaseth his good works.

56.

"There is no reward but Paradise for a Muslim who suffereth with patience when the soul of his affectionate friend is taken." What are those of your followers to do, who have lost no child? Lord Muhammad said, "Then am I as the child of them; and am going be-

---

ings of Ignorance', — loud lamentations, wailings, slapping the cheeks etc. — but not the silent grief of the heart.

fore, to prepare for their futurity; and this reward, which is for the death of their children, is on account of the pain and misfortune which they suffer; and they were never so stricken with misfortune like that which has attended my mission; for my followers love me more than they do their parents and children.

57.

Happy is the Mu'min, for, if good befalleth him, he praiseth and thanketh God; and, if misfortune, praiseth God and beareth it patiently; therefore a Mu'min is rewarded in every affair, even for his putting a mouthful of victuals into the mouth of his wife.

58.

And behold! a bier passed by Lord Muhammad, and he stood up; and it was said to him, "This is the bier of a Jew." He said, "Was it not the holder of a soul, from which we should take example and fear?"

59.

Death is a favour to a Muslim. Remember and speak well of your dead, and refrain from speaking ill of them.

60.

The Kur'ān consisteth of five heads, things lawful, things unlawful, clear and positive precepts, mysteries, and examples. Then consider that lawful which is there declared to be so, and that which is forbidden as unlawful; obey the precepts, believe in the mysteries, and take warning from the examples.

61.

Torment not yourselves, lest God should punish you.

62.

Verily ye are in an age in which if ye neglect one tenth of what is ordered, ye will be ruined. After this a time will come, when he who shall observe one tenth of what is now ordered will be redeemed.[1]

63.

Mankind will not go astray after having found the right road, unless from disputation.

64.

Whoever hath eaten of pure food and practised my laws, and mankind hath lived in security from him, will enter into the Abode of Bliss.

65.

The Messenger of God said to me (Anas), "Son, if you are able, keep your heart from morning till night and from night till morning, free from malice towards anyone;" then he said, "Oh! my son, this is one of my laws, and he who loveth my laws verily loveth me."

66.

"Verily the children of Israel were

---

1 *The promised time is the Dawn. Is not the Dawn at hand?*

separated into seventy-two tribes, and mine will be divided into seventy-three; every one of them will perish except one class." The companions said "Which is that one?" He said, "The religion which is professed by *me* and *my* friends."

67.

I admonish you to fear God, and yield obedience to my successor, although he may be a black slave, for this reason, that those amongst you who may live after me will see great schisms. Therefore hold fast my ways and those of my successors, who may be directors in the straight path, having found it themselves; and ardently seize my laws and be firm thereto.

68.

Doth anyone of you suppose that God hath not forbidden anything except in the Kur'ān? Beware, for verily I swear by God that I have ordered, and prohibited things in manner like the Kur'ān or more than it: and God hath not made it lawful for you to enter the houses of the People of the Book (that is Jews, Christians etc.) without their permission, or that you beat their women, or eat their fruits.

69.

Islām commenced in a forlorn state, and it will quickly return to what it was in the beginning; then be joyful ye who are firm.

70.

There was not any Messenger sent before me by God to mankind but found friends and companions, who embraced his maxims and became his disciples; after which were born those who gave out precepts which they did not practise, and did what they were not ordered to do: therefore those who oppose them with the hand, with the tongue, and with the heart are Mu'mins, and there is not anything in Imān besides this, even as much as a grain of mustard seed.

71.

Men will be liars towards the end of the world; and will relate such stories as neither you nor your fathers ever heard. Then avoid them, that they may not lead you astray and throw you into contention and strife.

72.

My religion is like clouds dropping much rain; some of them, falling on pure, favourable soil, cause fresh grass to grow; some of them fall in hollows from which mankind are benefited, some fall on high lands from which benefit is derived; then the two first are like the persons aquainted with the religion of God and instructing others; and the last like the person not regarding it nor accepting the right path.

73.

I am no more than man; when I order you anything respecting religion, receive it, and when I order you anything about the affairs of the world, then am I nothing more than man.

74.

The greatest enemies of God are those who are entered into Islam, and do acts of infidelity, and who, without cause, shed the blood of man.

75.

The grave is the first stage of the journey into eternity.

76.

Do not associate any one thing with God, although they kill or burn you; nor affront intentionally your parents, although they should order you to quit your wife, your children, and your property. Never drink wine; for it is the root of all evil; abstain from vice; and when a pestilence shall pervade mankind, and you shall be amongst them, remain with them; and cherish your children.

77.

Lord Muhammad said, "When a man committeth adultery, Imān (Faith) leaveth him; but when he leaveth such bad ways, Imān will return to him."

78.

There are three roots to Imān: one of them not to trouble him who shall say 'there is no deity but God'; not to think him an unbeliever on account of one fault; and not to discard him for one crime.

79.

Lord Muhammad said, "He is not a Mu'min (a Believer) who committeth adultery, or who stealeth, or who drinketh liquor, or who plundereth, or who embezzleth; beware, beware."

80.

Lord Muhammad said, "The greatest

crimes are to associate another with God, to vex your father and mother, to murder your own species, to commit suicide, and to swear to a lie."

81.

I asked Lord Muhammad of the most excellent Imān, and he said, "To love him who loveth God, and hate him who hateth God, and to keep your tongue employed in repeating the name of God." What else? He said, "To do unto all men as you would wish to have done unto you, and to reject for others what you would reject for yourself."

82.

What is Islām? I asked Lord Muhammad. He said, "Abstinence and Obedience." And then I asked him what was the most excellent Imān. He said, "An amiable disposition." Which is the most excellent Hijrah? He said, "Abandoning that which God disapproveth of."

---

1 See p. 11.

83.

What is Islām? I asked Lord Muhammad. He said, "Purity of speech and charity."

84.

A man asked Muhammad what was the mark whereby a man might know the reality of his faith. He said, "If thou derive pleasure from the good which thou hast performed, and be grieved for the evil which thou hast committed, thou art a true believer." The man said, "What doth a fault really consist in?" He said, "When anything pricketh thy conscience, forsake it."

85.

He who seeth me seeth the Truth.

86.

He who progresseth daily is yet of feeble mind (i. e. yet far off from the Ideal).

87.

People asked him (Muhammad) if to say, "There is no deity but God", was not the key of Paradise? He said, "Yes, but it is a key which hath wards, and if ye come with a key of that description, Paradise will be opened to you, otherwise it will not."

88.

Verily God doth not take away knowledge from the hands of his servants; but taketh it by taking away the learned; so that when no learned men remain, the ignorant will be placed at the head of affairs. Causes will be submitted to their decision, they will pass sentence without knowledge, will err themselves, and lead others into error.

89.

O Muhammad! Remember the Lord in retirement from the people and make prayer thy sleep, and hunger thy food.

90.

Kill not your hearts with excess of eating and drinking.

91.

The most excellent Jihād (Holy War) is that for the conquest of self.

92.

Illumine your hearts by hunger, and strive to conquer your self by hunger and thirst; continue to knock at the gates of Paradise by hunger.

93.

An hour's contemplation is better than a year's adoration.

94.

Charity is a duty unto every Muslim. He who hath not the means thereto, let him do a good act or abstain from an evil one. That is his charity.

95.

Almsgiving is a duty unto you. Alms should be taken from the rich and returned to the poor.

96.

He who believeth in one God and in a future life (i. e. a Muslim) let him honour his guest.

97.

Hell is veiled in delights, and Heaven in hardships and miseries.

98.

Do not speak ill of the dead.

99.

Every child is born with a disposition towards the natural religion (Islām). It is the parents who make it a Jew, a Christian or a Magian [1].

---

1 Hence according to Islām the souls of 'unbaptised' babes are not lost.

100.

Philosophy is the stray camel of the Faithful; take hold of it wherever ye come across it.

101.

Go in quest of knowledge even unto China.[1]

102.

Seek knowledge from the cradle to the grave.

103.

Prayer is the mi'rāj (union with, or annihilation in, the Divine Essence by means of continual upward progress) of the Faithful.

104.

All actions are judged by the motives prompting them.

105.

Heaven lieth at the feet of mothers.

---

1 i. e., even unto the 'edge of the earth'.

106.

The Lord doth not regard a prayer in which the heart doth not accompany the body.

107.

He whom prayer preventeth not from wrongdoing and evil, increaseth in naught save in remoteness from the Lord.

108.

The love of the world is the root of all evils.

109.

When you speak, speak the truth; perform when you promise; discharge your trust; commit not fornication; be chaste; have no impure desires; withhold your hands from striking, and from taking that which is unlawful and bad. The best of God's servants are those who, when seen, remind of God; and the worst of God's servants are those who carry tales about, to do mischief and separate friends, and seek for the defects of the good.

110.

If the unbeliever knew of the extent of the Lord's mercy, even he would not despair of Paradise.

111.

He who believeth in one God and the Hereafter (i. e. a Muslim) let him speak what is good or remain silent.

112.

He who believeth in one God and the life beyond (i. e. a Muslim) let him not injure his neighbours.

113.

Speak to men according to their mental capacities, for if you speak all things to all men, some cannot understand you, and so fall into errors.

114.

The son of Man groweth and with him grow two things — the love of wealth and love of long life.

115.

Everyone is divinely furthered in accordance with his character.

116.

It is your own conduct which will lead you to reward or punishment, as if you had been destined therefor.

117.

Every human being hath two inclinations — one prompting him to good and impelling him thereto, and the other prompting him to evil and thereto impelling him; but Divine assistance is nigh, and he who asketh the help of God in contending with the evil promptings of his own heart obtaineth it.

118.

"By what rule" said Lord Muhammad, "would you be guided, O Mu'āz, in your administration of Yemen?" "By the law of the Kur'ān." "But if you find no direction in the Kur'ān?" "Then I will act according to the example of the Messenger of God." "But if that faileth?" "Then I will exercise my own reason and judgment."

119.

It is not a sixth or a tenth of a man's devotion which is acceptable to God, but only such portions thereof as he offereth with understanding and true devotional spirit.

120.

Verily these your deeds will be brought back to you, as if you yourself were the creator of your own punishment.

121.

Death is a bridge that uniteth friend with friend.

122.

This world is a prison for the Faithful, but a Paradise for unbelievers.

123.

Cursed is this world and cursed is all that is in this world, except the remembrance of God and that which aideth it.

124.

The world is a magician, greater than Hārūt and Mārūt, and you should avoid it.

125.

God's kindness towards His creatures is more than a mother's towards her babe.

126.

Adore God as thou wouldst if thou sawest Him; for, if thou seest Him not, He seeth thee.

127.

Sleep is the brother of death.

128.

My people will, in the eternal life, rise up in companies — that is, some as apes, some as tigers, some as hogs, etc., (according to the ruling passion of their earthly lives).

129.

Poverty is my pride.

130.

Lord Muhammad said one day to his companions, "Reverence God as becometh you." They said, "Verily, O Apostle of God, we do reverence Him, and praise be to God who hath endued us with it." Then Lord Muhammad said, "It is not so; but whoever reverenceth God as it is suitable for him to do, must guard his head from humbling itself to others, and from pride and arrogance towards God and God's creatures; he must guard his senses from whatever is wrong, and must guard his mouth from eating forbidden things, and his heart from receiving what is prohibited; and he must keep death in mind, and the rotting of his bones. And whoever wisheth for future rewards must abandon the ornaments of the world. Therefore, anyone attending to the aforementioned points has verily reverenced God as it is his duty to do."

131.

I heard the Messenger of God say, (three days before his death): "Not one of you must die but with resignation to the will of God, and with hope for his beneficence and pardon."

132.

Remember often the destroyer and cutter off of delights, which is death.

133.

Not one of you must wish for death, from any worldly affliction; but if there certainly is anyone wishing for death, he must say, "O Lord, keep me alive so long as life may be good for me, and cause me to die when it is better for me so to do."

134.

When the bier of anyone passeth by you, whether Jew, Christian, or Muslim, rise to thy feet.

135.

We came with Lord Muhammad to Abū Yūsuf, a blacksmith; and he was the husband of the nurse of Ibrahīm. And the Apostle of God took Ibrahīm and kissed him and smelt him. Afterwards we came to him, when he was in his dying moments. Then the eyes of Lord Muhammad were fixed, and flowed with tears; and 'Abd-al-Raḥmān son of 'Auf said to the Messenger of God, "Do you weep and shed tears, O Apostle of God?" He said, "O son of 'Auf, these tears are compassion, and feeling due to the dead." After that he shed tears again, and said, "Verily my eyes shed tears and my heart is afflicted, and I say nothing but what is pleasing to my Benefactor; for verily, O Ibrahīm, I am melancholy at being separated from thee."

136.

Said Lord Muhammad, "Now, the adultery of the eye is to look with an eye of desire on the wife of another; and the adultery of the tongue is to utter what is forbidden."

137.

God doth not remove anyone out of

the world, but that He wisheth to pardon him; and by the diseases of his body and distress for food, He exacteth the punishment of every fault that lieth on his shoulder. (That is, by suffering in this world, he is exempted from punishment in the next).

138.

Ye followers of Muhammad, I swear by God, there is not anything which God so abhors, as his male and female servants committing adultery.

139.

Verily the greatness of rewards is as the greatness of misfortune; that is, whoever is most unfortunate and calamitous, the greater and more perfect his reward. And verily, when God loveth a people, he entangleth it in misfortune; therefore, he who is resigned to the pleasure of God, in misfortune, for him is God's pleasure.

140.

Verily Lord Muhammad said, "No misfortune or vexation befalleth a servant, small or great, but on account of his faults committed; and most of these God forgiveth."

141.

There is not any Muslim who visiteth another in sickness, in the forenoon, but that seventy thousand angels send blessings upon him till the evening; and there is no one who visiteth the sick, in the afternoon, but that seventy thousand angels send blessings upon him till daybreak, and there will be a pardon for him in Paradise.

142.

Feed the hungry and visit the sick, and free the captive, if he be unjustly confined. Assist any person oppressed, whether Muslim or non-Muslim.

143.

"The duties of Muslims to each other are six". It was asked "What are they, O Messenger of God?" He said, "When you meet a Muslim salaam to him, and when he inviteth you to dinner, accept; and when he asketh you for advice, give it him; and when he sneezeth and saith 'Praise be to God', do you say 'May God have mercy upon thee; and when he is sick, visit him; and when he dieth, follow his bier."

144.

Whoever visiteth a sick person, an angel calleth from heaven, "Be happy in the world, and happy be your walking, and take you a habitation in Paradise."

Whoever visiteth a sick person always entereth into and swims in a sea of mercy until he sitteth down; and when he sitteth, he is drowned therein.

145.

When you go to visit the sick,

comfort his grief, and say, "You will get well and live long," because this saying will not prevent what is predestined, but it will solace his soul.

146.

Verily when a Muslim is taken ill, after which God restoreth him to health, his illness hath been a cover to his former faults, and it is an admonition to him of what cometh in future times; and verily, when a hypocrite is taken ill, and afterwards restored to health, he is like a camel which hath been tied up, and afterwards set free; for the camel did not know for want of discrimination, why they tied him up and why they let him loose; such is the hypocrite; on the contrary, a Mu'min knoweth, that his indisposition was to cover his faults.

147.

Misfortune is always with the Muslim and his wife, either in their persons or their property or children; either death or sickness; until they die, when there is no fault upon them.

148.

This life is but a tillage for the next, do good that you may reap there; for striving is the ordinance of God, and whatever God hath ordained can only be attained by striving.

149.

Every eye is an adulterer; and whatever woman perfumeth herself, and goeth to an assembly where men are, wishing to show herself to them, with a look of lasciviousness, is an adulteress. (That is, every eye that looks with desire upon a woman commits adultery).

150.

Lord Muhammad used to say, after making the profession of faith, "O Lord, I supplicate Thee for firmness in faith, and inclination towards the straight path, and for Thine aid in being grateful to Thee, and in adoring Thee in every good way; and I supplicate Thee for an innocent heart which shall not incline to wickedness; and I supplicate Thee for a true tongue, and for that virtue which Thou knowest to be so, and to defend me from that vice which Thou knowest to be so; and for forgiveness of those faults which Thou knowest."

151.

Verily the Messenger of God said to his companions, "What are your opinions of the merits of that person, who drinketh liquor, committeth adultery, and stealeth? What should his punishment be?" They said, "God and His Messenger know best." He said, "These are great sins, and the punishment for them very dire." (This question was asked before the precepts in the Kur'ān, in which those things are forbidden, descended).

152.

I said, "O Messenger of God, permit me to become a eunuch." He said, "That person is not of me who maketh another a eunuch, or becometh so himself; because the manner in which my followers become eunuchs is by fasting and abstinence." I then said, "Permit me to retire from society, and to abandon the delights of the world." He said, "The retirement that becometh my followers is to live in the world and yet to sit in the corner of a mosque in expectation of prayers."

153.

The knowledge from which no benefit is derived is like a treasure from which no charity is bestowed in the way of the Lord.

154.

The Messenger of God repeated

something of strife and said, "It will appear at the time of knowledge leaving the world." I said, "O Messenger of God, how will knowledge go from the world, since we read the Kur'ān, and teach it to our children, and our children to theirs; and so on till the last day?" Then Lord Muhammad said, "O Zīād, I supposed you the most learned man of Medinah. *Do the Jews and Christians who read the Bible and the Evangel act on them?*"

155.

I received from the Messenger of God, two kinds of knowledge; one of these I taught to others, and if I had taught them the other, it would have broken their throats.

156.

Do you know what sappeth the foundations of Islām, and ruineth it? The errors of the learned destroy it, and the disputations of the hypocrite, and the orders of kings who have lost the road.

157.

Women are the twin-halves of men.

158.

There are seven people whom God will draw under His own shadow, on the day when there will be no other shadow; one of them, a man who hath given alms and concealed it, so that his left hand knew not what his right hand did.

159.

A Bedouin was standing in the mosque of the Prophet, and defiled it; when he was immediately taken hold of; and the Messenger of God said "Let him alone, and throw a skin of water upon the spot; because ye were not created but as comforters and not sent to create hardships." And they let him alone till he had done, and then Lord Muhammad called the 'Arābi to him, and said, "This mosque is not a proper place for that, or any kind of filth; mosques are only for the mention of God, saying prayers and reading the Kur'ān."

160.

The key of Paradise is prayer, and the key of prayer is ablution.

161.

The calamity of knowledge is forgetfulness; and to lose knowledge is this, to speak of it to the unworthy.

Who are the learned? Those who practise what they know.

162.

The time is near in which nothing will remain of Islām but its name, and of the Kur'ān but its mere appearance, and the mosques of Muslims will be destitute of knowledge and worship; and the learned men will be the worst people under the heavens; and contention and strife will issue from them, and it will return upon themselves.

163.

Excessive knowledge is better than excessive praying; and the support of religion is abstinence.

It is better to teach knowledge one hour in the night, than to pray the whole night.

164.

Whoever seeketh knowledge and findeth it, will get two rewards; one of them the reward for desiring it, and the other for attaining it; therefore, even if he do not attain it, for him is one reward.

165.

That person who shall die while he

is studying knowledge, in order to revive the knowledge of religion, will be only one degree inferior to the prophets.

166.

The Kur'ān was sent down in seven dialects; and in every one of its sentences, there is an external and internal meaning.

167.

One learned man is harder on the devil, than a thousand ignorant worshippers.

The desire of knowledge is a divine commandement for every Muslim; and to instruct in knowledge those who are unworthy of it is like putting pearls, jewels, and gold on the necks of swine.

168.

Verily I heard Lord Muhammad say, "That person who shall pursue the path of knowledge, God will direct him to the path of Paradise; and verily the superiority of a learned man over an ignorant worshipper is like that of the full moon over all the stars."

169.

Ye followers of Muhammad, I swear by the Lord, if ye did but know what I know of the future state, verily ye would laugh little and cry much.

170.

The best of good acts in God's sight is that which is constantly attended to, although in a small degree.

171.

Commandments are of three kinds: one, the reward of which is clear, then follow it; one, which leads astray, abstain from it; and another in which arise contradictions, resign that to God.

172.

The world is forbidden to those of

the life to come; the life to come is forbidden to those of this world; and both are forbidden to the true servants of God.

173.

The Faithful do not die; perhaps they become translated from this perishable world to the world of eternal existences.

174.

Do a good deed after every bad deed that it may blot out the latter.

175.

He who knoweth his own self, knoweth God.

176.

Convey to other persons none of my words, except those ye know of a surety.

177.

My sayings do not abrogate the word of God but the word of God can abrogate my sayings.

178.

Of my disciples that will enter Paradise are those who do not use shells, and are not influenced by omens, like the people of Ignorance, and who put their whole trust in God.

179.

A true Mu'min is thankful to God in prosperity, and resigned to His will in adversity.

180.

If you put your whole trust in God, as you ought, He most certainly will give you sustenance, as He doth the birds; they come out hungry in the morning, but return full to their nests.

181.

Trust in God, but tie your camel.

182.

Beware! verily there is a piece of flesh in the body of man, which, when good, the whole body is good; and, when bad, the whole body is bad, and that is the heart.

183.

Lord Muhammad said to me, 'O Wābīṣah! are you come to ask what is goodness and what is badness?' I said, 'Yes, I am come for that.' Then he oined his fingers and struck them upon my breast, that is made a sign towards my heart, and said, 'Ask the sentence from thine own heart.' This he repeated three times and said, "Goodness is a thing from which thy heart findeth firmness and rest; and badness is a thing which throweth thee into doubt, although men may acquit thee."

184.

Whoso hath left debt and children, let them come to me; I am their patron, I will discharge his debt and befriend his children.

185.

It beseemeth me to be kinder to Muslims than they to each other; wherefore any Muslim dying in debt, and not leaving property to discharge it, it resteth with me; and whoso leaveth property, it is for his heirs.

186.

Marriage is incumbent on all who possess the ability.

187.

There is no monasticism in Islām.

188.

S'ad b. Abi Wakkās said: 'The Apostle forbade 'Uthmān b. Ma'ẓūn from avoiding marriage: and if he had permitted that to him, verily we (the other Muslims) would have become eunuchs.'

189.

A woman may be married by four qualifications: one on account of her money; another, on account of the nobility of her pedigree; another, on account of her beauty; the fourth, on account of her virtue. Therefore, look out for a woman that hath virtue: but if you do it from any other consideration, your hands be rubbed in dirt.

190.

The world and all things in it are valuable; but the most valuable thing in the world is a virtuous woman.

191.

The best women in Arabia are the virtuous of the Kuraish; they are the most affectionate to infants, and they are the most careful of their husbands' property.

192.

The world is sweet in the heart, and green to the eye; and verily God hath brought you, after those that went before you: then look to your actions, and abstain from the world and its wickedness.

193.

Admonish your wives with kindness.

194.

A Muslim must not hate his wife; and if he be displeased with one bad quality in her, then let him be pleased with another which is good.

195.

Do you beat your own wife as you would a slave? That must you not do.

196.

The best of you, before God and his creation, are those who are best in their own families, and I am the best to my family. When your friend dieth, mention not his vices.

197.

When a woman performeth the five

times of prayer, and fasteth the month of Ramaḍān, and is chaste, and is not disobedient to her husband, then tell her to enter Paradise by whichever door she liketh.

198.

I (Mu'āvīyah b. Ḥaidah) said, 'O Apostle of God! what is my duty to my wife?' He said, 'That you give her to eat when you eat yourself, and clothe her when you clothe yourself; and do not slap her in the face nor abuse her, nor separate yourself from her in displeasure.'

199.

Give your wife good counsel; and if she has goodness in her, she will soon take it, and leave off idle talking; and do not beat your noble wife like a slave.

200.

Lord Muhammad said: "Beat not your

wives." Then Omar came to the Rasūl and said, 'Wives have got the upper hand of their husbands from hearing this.'

201.

Verily a great number of women are assembled near my family, complaining of their husbands; and those men who beat their wives do not behave well. He is not of my way who teacheth a woman to stray.

202.

He is of the most perfect Muslims, whose disposition is most liked by his own family.

203.

That is the most perfect Muslim whose disposition is best; and the best of you are they, who behave best to their wives.

204.

Kais b. S'ad said: "I came to Ḥīrah,

and saw the inhabitants worshipping their chief; and I said, 'Verily the Apostle of God is worthy of being worshipped.' Then I came to the Apostle and said, 'I saw the people of Ḥīrah worshipping the chief of their tribe, and you are most worthy of being worshipped.' Then Lord Muhammad said to me 'Tell me that if you should pass by my grave, would you worship it?' I said 'No'. And he said 'Worship not me.'"

205.

The Apostle was in the midst of a crowd of his companions, and a camel came and prostrated itself before him. They said, 'O Apostle of God! beasts and trees worship thee; then it is meet for us to worship thee'. Lord Muhammad said, 'Worship God, and you may honour your brother, that is, me.'

206.

Every woman who asketh to be divorced from her husband without cause, the fragrance of the Garden is forbidden her.

207.

The thing which is lawful, but disliked by God, is divorce.

208.

O Apostle of God! How many times are we to forgive our servants' faults? He was silent. Again the questioner asked, and Lord Muhammad gave no answer. But when the man asked a third time, he said, 'Forgive your servants seventy times a day.'

209.

To those of your servants who please you give to eat what you eat yourself; and clothe them as yourself; but those who do not please you, part with them; and punish not God's creatures.

210.

Fear God, in these dumb animals

and ride them when they are fit to be rode and get off them when they are tired.

211.

Shall I tell you the very worst amongst you? Those who eat alone, and whip the slaves, and give to nobody.

212.

He will not enter Paradise who, behaveth ill to his slaves. The companions said, 'O Apostle of God! Have you not told us, that there will be a great many slaves and orphans amongst your disciples?' He said, 'Yes; then be kind to them and to your own children, and give them to eat of what you eat yourselves. The slaves that say their prayers are your brothers.'

213.

There is no man who is wounded and pardoneth the giver of the wound but God will exalt his dignity and diminish his faults.

214.

Verily the best of God's servants are just and learned kings; and verily the worst are bad and ignorant kings.

215.

Whoever believeth in God and the Hereafter (i. e. a Muslim), must respect his guest: and whoever believeth in God and the Hereafter, must not incommode his neighbours; and a Mu'min must speak only good words, otherwise remain silent.

216.

It is not right for a guest to stay so long as to incommode his host.

217.

O Apostle of God! Inform me, if I stop with a man, and he doth not entertain me, and he afterwards stoppeth at my house, am I to entertain him or act with him as he did with me? Lord Muhammad said, 'Entertain him.'

218.

Being confined for room, the Apostle of God sat down upon his legs drawn up under his thighs. A desert Arab who was present said, 'What is this way of sitting?' Lord Muhammad said, 'Verily God hath made me a humble slave, and not a proud king.'

219.

When victuals are placed, no man must stand up till it be taken away; nor must one man leave off eating before the rest; and if he doeth, he must make an apology.

220.

Imām Ja'far Ṣādik said, 'The Apostle used, when he ate in company, to eat to the last, and did not leave off before others.'

221.

It is of my ways that a man shall come out with his guest to the door of his house.

222.

Asmā', daughter of Yazīd, said, 'Victuals were brought to Lord Muhammad, and he put them before some of us women who were present, and said, 'Eat ye.' But notwithstanding we were hungry we said, 'We have no inclination.' Lord Muhammad said, 'O women! do not mix hunger with lies.'

223.

You will not enter Paradise until you have faith; and you will not complete your faith till you love one another.

224.

'Ā'ishah said, "A party of Jews asked permission to go to Lord Muhammad, and said, 'Death upon you'[1]. And I answered their salutation by saying 'Rather upon you be death and curse'. Then Lord Muhammad said, 'Be mild, O 'Ā'ishah! and make a point of being kind, and withhold thyself from speaking harshly.' I said, 'Did you not hear what they said?' He said, "Verily, I do always say, 'Be the same to you.'"

225.

Some eloquence is like magic.

226.

Some poetry is dressed in knowledge and art.

227.

The truest words spoken by any poet are those of Labīd: 'Know that everything is vanity save God'.

---

1 Whilst saluting the Muslims the Jews used to 'twist their tongues' and wish them 'death' (السأم) instead of 'peace' (السلام), words which have a similarity of sound in Arabic.

228.

Meekness and modesty are two branches of Imān; and vain talking and embellishing are two branches of hypocrisy.

229.

Verily the most beloved of you by me, and nearest to me in the next world, are those of good dispositions; and verily the greatest enemies to me and the farthest from me, are the ill-tempered.

230.

Some eloquence is magic; and verily some knowledge is a cause of ignorance; and some poetry is philosophy; and verily some speeches are heavy.

231.

Abusing a Muslim is disobedience to God; and it is infidelity to fight with one.

232.

Every man who calls a Muslim infidel, it will return upon him.

233.

It is not worthy of a speaker of truth to curse people.

234.

Appropriate to yourselves the truth. Avoid lying.

235.

It is unworthy of a Mu'min to injure people's reputations; and it is unworthy to curse any one; and it is unworthy to abuse any one; and it is unworthy of a Mu'min to talk vainly.

236.

It is better to sit alone than in company with the bad; and it better to sit with the good than alone. And it is better to speak words to a seeker of knowledge than to remain silent; and silence is better than bad words.

237.

Fear not the obloquy of the detractor in showing God's religion.

238.

Say what is true, although it may be bitter and displeasing to people.

239.

Refrain from seeing and speaking of the vices of mankind, which you know are in yourself.

240.

Much silence and a good disposition, there are no two works better than those.

241.

Guard yourselves from six things, and I am your security for Paradise. When you speak, speak the truth; perform when you promise; discharge your trust; be chaste in thought and action; and withhold your hand from striking, from taking that which is unlawful, and bad.

242.

Backbiting vitiates ablution and fasting.

243.

Do not exceed bounds in praising me, as the Christians do in praising Jesus, the son of Mary, by calling him God, and the Son of God; I am only the Lord's servant; then call me the servant of God, and His messenger.

244.

Verily God instructs me to be humble and lowly and not proud; and that no one should oppress another.

245.

A tribe must desist from boasting of their forefathers: if they will not leave off boasting, verily they will be more abominable near God, than a black beetle which rolleth on filth by its nose; and verily God has removed from you pride and arrogance. There is no man but either a righteous Mu'min or a sinner: mankind are all the sons of Adam, and he was from earth.

246.

I went along with the ambassadors of Bani 'Āmir to Lord Muhammad; and we said, 'You are our master.' He said, 'God is your master.' Then we said, 'You are most excellent of the highest degree.' And when he heard this, he said, 'Say so, or less, and do not exceed reasonable bounds in praise'.

247.

That person is not of us who inviteth others to aid him in oppression; and he is not of us who fighteth for his tribe in injustice; and he is not of us who dieth in assisting his tribe in tyranny.

248.

Your loving a thing maketh you deaf and blind (i. e. love is blind).

249.

He is not a perfect performer of propinquity who doeth good to his relatives as they do to him; but he is perfect who doeth good to them when they do it not to him.

250.

God's pleasure is in a father's pleasure; and God's displeasure is in a father's displeasure.

251.

The favour of God doth not descend upon that family in which is one who deserts his relations.

252.

He who wisheth to enter Paradise, at the best door must please his father and mother.

253.

O Messenger of God! verily I have done a great crime; is there any act by which I may repent? He said, 'Have you a mother? 'No', said the questioner. 'Have you an aunt?' asked Muhammad. He said, 'Yes, I have'. Lord Muhammad said, 'Go do good to her, and your crime will be pardoned'.

254.

I saw Lord Muhammad distributing meat in Ji'rānah; and behold a woman came close to him, and he spread his garment for her to sit upon. When I saw such respect shown to the woman, I asked who she was; and those present said, 'This is his nurse.'

255.

A man is bound to do good to his parents, although they may have injured him.

256.

There is no child, a doer of good to his parents, who looketh on them with kindness and affection, but God will write for every look as the rewards for an approved pilgrimage.

257.

The duty of a junior to a senior brother is as that of a child to its father.

258.

God is not merciful to him who is not so to mankind.

259.

Whoever doeth good to girls, it will be a curtain to him from hell-fire.

260.

Whoever befriendeth two girls till they come of age, will be in the next world along with me, like my two fingers joining each other.

261.

A giver of maintenance to widows and the poor, is like a bestower in the road of God, an utterer of prayers all the night, and a keeper of constant fast.

262.

I and the guardian of orphans (whether the orphan be of his near or distant relations, or of strangers) will be in one place in the next world; like my two fingers, nearly touching each other.

263.

All Muslims are as one person. If a man complaineth of a pain in his head, his whole body complaineth; and if his eye complaineth, his whole body complaineth.

264.

All Muslims are like one foundation, some parts strengthening others; in such a way must they support each other.

265.

Assist your brother Muslim, whether he be an oppressor or an oppressed. 'But how shall we do it when he is an oppressor?' Lord Muhammad said, 'Assisting an oppressor is by forbidding and withholding him from oppression.'

266.

Muslims are brothers in religion and they must not oppress one another, nor abandon assisting each other, nor hold one another in contempt. The seat of righteousness is the heart; therefore that heart which is righteous, does not hold a Muslim in contempt: and all the things of one Muslim are unlawful to another; his blood, property and reputation.

267.

No man hath believed perfectly, until he wish for his brother that which he wisheth for himself.

268.

When three persons are together, two of them must not whisper to each other without letting the third hear, until others are present, because it would hurt him.

269.

Religion is admonition; and it means being pure.

270.

Kindness is a mark of faith, and whoever hath not kindness hath not faith.

271.

Whoever is kind to the creation, God is kind to him; therefore be kind to man on the earth, whether he be good or bad; and being kind to the bad, is to withhold them from badness.

272.

He is not of us who is not affectionate to the little ones and doth not respect the reputation of the old; and he is not of us who doth not order that which is lawful, and prohibit that which is unlawful.

273.

Verily, it is one of the respects to God, to honour an old man.

274.

The best Muslim house is that in which is an orphan, who is benefited; and the worst Muslim house is that in which is an orphan ill-treated.

275.

Whoever befriendeth three daughters, or three sisters, and teacheth them manners, and is affectionate to them, till they come of age, may God apportion Paradise for him.

276.

Verily, a man teaching his child manners is better for him than giving one bushel of grain in alms.

277.

No father hath given his child anything better than good manners.

278.

I and a woman whose colour and cheeks shall have become black shall be near to one another in the next world as my two fingers; and that is a handsome widow, whose colour and cheeks shall have become black in bringing up her family.

279.

Whoever hath a daughter, and doth not bury her alive, or scold her, or shew partiality to his other children, may God bring him into Paradise.

280.

Verily, each of you is a mirror to his brother: then if he seeth a vice in his brother he must tell him to get rid of it.

281.

The best person in God's sight is the best amongst his friends; and the best of neighbours near God is the best person in his own neighbourhood.

282.

Respect people agreeably to their eminence.

283.

That person is not a perfect Muslim who eateth his fill, and leaveth his neighbours hungry.

284.

The exercise of religious duties will not atone for the fault of an abusive tongue.

285.

A man cannot be a Muslim till his heart and tongue are so [1].

---

1 The Islām of heart is its purity; and the Islām of the tongue withholding it from fruitless words.

286.

The creation is as God's family; for its sustenance is from him: therefore the most beloved unto God is the person who doeth good to God's family.

287.

Shall I not point out to you the best of virtues? It is your doing good to your daughter when she is returned to you having been divorced by her husband.

288.

Souls, before having dependence upon bodies, were like assembled armies; after that they were dispersed; and sent into bodies. Therefore, those which were acquainted before the dependence attract each other, and those that were unacquainted, repel.

289.

Shall I not inform you of a better

act than fasting, alms, and prayers? Making peace between one another: enmity and malice tear up rewards by the roots.

290.

Keep yourselves far from envy; because it eateth up and taketh away good actions, like as fire eateth up and burneth wood.

291.

O ye who have embraced Islām by the tongue, and to whose hearts it hath not reached, distress not Muslims, nor speak ill of them, nor seek for their defects.

292.

It is near that poverty will become a cause of infidelity.

293.

Verily you [1] have two qualities which

---

1 Ashbaḥ, chief of the embassy from ʿAbd-al-kais.

God and His messenger love, — fortitude and gentleness.

294.

Deliberation in undertakings is pleasing to God.

295.

He is not a perfect man of fortitude, who hath not fallen into misfortunes; and there is no physician but the experienced.

296.

A good disposition, and deliberation in works, and a medium in all things, are one part of twenty four parts of prophecy; I mean they are of the qualities of the prophets.

297.

God hath not created anything better than Reason, or any thing more perfect, or more beautiful than Reason; the benefits which God giveth are on its account; and understanding is by it, and God's wrath [1] is caused by it, and by it are rewards and punishments.

298.

Verily, a man hath performed prayers, fasts, charity, pilgrimage and all other good works; but he will not be rewarded but by the proportion of his sense.

299.

Verily, God is mild, and is fond of mildness, and he giveth to the mild what he doth not to the harsh.

300.

All kinds of modesty are best.

301.

Verily, the most beloved of you by me are those of the best dispositions.

---

1 I. e., 'rational' (voluntary) action is the object of moral judgment.

302.

Whoever hath been given gentleness hath been given a good portion, in this world and the next.

303.

The proud will not enter Paradise, nor a violent speaker.

304.

A Muslim who mixeth with people and putteth up with their inconveniences, is better than one who doth not mix with them, and bear with patience.

305.

Whoever suppresseth his anger, when he hath in his power to shew it, God will give him a great reward.

306.

May God fill the heart of that person who suppresseth his anger with safety and faith.

307.

Mu'āz said, "At the time of my being despatched to the judgeship of Yemen, the last advice Lord Muhammad gave me was this, 'O Mu'āz! be of good temper towards people'.

308.

I have been sent to explain fully good dispositions.

309.

O Lord! as thou hast made my figure good, so make good my disposition.

310.

Every man who shall beg, in order to increase his property, God will diminish it.

311.

Give me advice. Lord Muhammad said, 'Be not angry.'

312.

He is not strong and powerful, who throweth people down; but he is strong who withholdeth himself from anger.

313.

He will not enter hell, who hath faith equal to a single grain of mustard seed in his heart; and he will not enter paradise, who hath a single grain of pride, equal to one of mustard seed in his heart.

314.

Muhammad said: 'That person will not enter Paradise who hath one atom of pride in his heart.'

And a man present said, 'Verily, a man is fond of having good clothes, and good shoes.' Lord Muhammad said, 'God is Beauty and delighteth in the beautiful; and pride is holding man in contempt.'

315.

An old adulterer, a lying king, and a proud dervise are accursed.

316.

No person hath drunk a better draught than that of anger which he hath swallowed for God's sake.

317.

Whoever is humble to men for God's sake, may God exalt his eminence.

318.

That person is most respectable near God, who pardoneth, when he hath him in his power, him who shall have injured him.

319.

Do not say, that if people do good to us, we will do good to them; and if people oppress us, we will oppress them; but determine, that if people do you good, you will do good to them; and if they oppress you, you will not oppress them.

320.

There are two benefits, of which the generality of men are losers, and which they do not know the value of; one health, the other leisure.

321.

Verily, of things which I fear for you, after my departure from the world, is this: that the ornaments and goods of the world may be pleasing to you. Then a man said, 'O Messenger of God! doth good bring harm?' Lord Muhammad said, 'Verily good doth not bring harm: I mean if there be much wealth, it is of the number of benefits; and there is no harm in it, unless from stinginess and extravagance; like the spring, which causeth nothing to grow but what is good: and harm and destruction are from excess in eating.

322.

O Lord! give the family of Muhammad the necessaries of life.

323.

Riches are not from abundance of worldly goods, but from a contented mind.

324.

Teach me a work, such that when I perform it God and men will love me. Lord Muhammad said: Desire not the world, and God will love you; and desire not what men have, and they will love you.

325.

Lord Muhammad slept upon a mat, and got up very marked on the body by it: and I said, 'O messenger of God!

if thou hadst ordered me, I would have spread a soft bed for thee.' Lord Muhammad said, 'What business have I with the world? My condition with the world is that of a man on horseback, who standeth under the shade of a tree, then leaveth it.'

326.

The friend I most emulate is a Muslim unencumbered; I mean of small family, and little money; and a performer of prayers; and a perfect worshipper of God in private; who is unknown, and hath enough to supply his wants, and dieth soon, with few women crying for him, and few legacies.

327.

It is difficult, for a man laden with riches, to climb the steep path that leadeth to bliss.

328.

Can any one walk over water without

wetting his feet? The companions said, 'No'; Lord Muhammad said, 'Such is the condition of those of the world; they are not safe from sins.'

329.

Whoever desireth the world and its riches, in a lawfull manner, in order to withhold himself from begging, and for a livelihood for his family, and for being kind to his neighbour, will come to God with his face bright as the full moon, on the fourteenth night.

330.

In prayers, all thoughts must be laid aside, but those of God; in conversation, no word to be uttered which may afterwards be repented of; do not covet from others, or have any hopes from them.

331.

When Lord Muhammad sent me to Yemen, in a judicial capacity, he came out to take leave of me, and advise me and I was riding, and he was walking by the side of my camel, and when he had finished advice, he said, 'O Mu'āz! verily you will not find me after this year.' Then I wept, from sorrow, at being separated from him. Then he turned aside, and wept; and turned his face to Medinah; and said, '*The nearest to me are the abstinent, whoever they be, wherever they be.*'

332.

The people of Lord Muhammad's house did not eat their fill of barley bread, two days successively, as long as he lived. *'Ā'ishah.*

333.

I took barley bread and mutton to Lord Muhammad, and he had pawned his coat of mail with a Jew, and had taken a little barley from him for his family; and there never remained, any one night, a measure of barley, or any other grain, in his house, notwithstanding he had a family of nine. *Anas.*

334.

When you see a person, who hath been given more than you, in money and beauty; then look to those who hath been given less.

335.

Look to those inferior to yourselves; which is best for you, that you may not hold God's benefits in contempt.

336.

O Lord! Keep me alive a poor man, and let me die poor; and raise me amongst the poor.

337.

O 'Ā'ishah! do not turn the poor away, without giving them, if but half a date.

338.

Seek for my satisfaction in that of the poor and needy.

339.

The world is as a prison and as a famine to Muslims; and when they leave it you may say they leave famine and a prison.

340.

There are two things disliked by the sons of Adam, one of them death: whereas it is better for Muslims than sinning; the second is scarcity of money: whereas its account will be small in futurity.

341.

A man came to Lord Muhammad and said, 'Verily I love you.' He said, 'Look to what you say.' And the man said, 'By God! I love you', and repeated the same thrice. Lord Muhammad said, 'If you are sincere, then prepare armour for poverty; for poverty reacheth him who loveth me quicker than a torrent to the sea.'

342.

Three are the things of your world I am fond of—perfumes and the society of women, but that which my heart rejoiceth in is prayer.

343.

Verily God loveth a Muslim who is poor, with a family, and withholdeth himself from the unlawful and begging.

344.

Be in the world like a traveller, or like a passer on, and reckon yourself as of the dead.

345.

What is the best man? Lord Muhammad said, 'He is the best man whose life is long and his actions good.' Then who is the worst? 'Whose life is long and his actions bad.'

346.

Whoso openeth unto himself the door of begging, God will open unto him the door of poverty.

347.

That person is wise and sensible who subdueth his carnal desires and hopeth for rewards; and he is an ignorant man who followeth his lustful appetites, and with all this asketh God's forgiveness.

348.

Wealth, properly employed is a blessing; and a man may lawfully endeavour to increase it by honest means.

349.

When the Messenger of God entered a place of worship he used to say, 'O God! pardon my sins, and open for me the gates of thy compassion'; and when he left it he would repeat the same.

350.

Say your prayers standing; but if you are not able, do it sitting; and if not sitting, on your sides.

351.

Do none enter the Garden of Bliss save by God's mercy? Lord Muhammad said, 'No. None enter save through God's favour.' You also, O Messenger of God! Will you not enter Paradise save by God's compassion? Lord Muhammad put his hand on his head and said thrice, 'I also shall not enter unless God cover me with His mercy.'

352.

I am the City of Knowledge and 'Alī is the Bāb (Gate) thereof.

353.

Verily God will say, 'O children of Adam! I was sick and ye did not visit me.' And the sons of Adam will say, 'O our defender, how could we visit thee? For thou art the Lord of the Universe, and art free from sickness.' And God will say, 'O men! such a one was sick and you did not visit him.' And God will say, 'O children of Adam, I asked you for food, and ye gave it me not?' And the children of Adam will say, 'O our patron, how could we give thee food, seeing thou art the cherisher of the Universe, and art free from hunger and eating?' And God will say, 'Such a one asked you for bread and you did not give it him.'

354.

When any one of us was sick the Messenger of God used to rub his hands upon the sick person's body saying,

'O Lord of mankind! take away this pain, and give health; for thou art the giver of health: there is no health but thine, that health which leaveth no sickness.'

355.

When any person complained of being out of order, or having a wound, or sore, the Rasūl used to moisten his finger, and put it upon the earth, after which he would apply it to the painful part and rub it, saying, 'In the name of God; we have done this in order to restore the sick to health, by the permission of our Lord [1].'

356.

Whatever mishap may befall you, it

---

1 This is one of the secrets, says the commentator, which surpasses our sense and understanding.

is on account of something which your hands have done.

357.

God enjoins you to treat woman well, for they are your mothers, daughters, and aunts.

358.

I saw the Messenger of God in his dying moments, and there was a cup near him in which was water, and he put his hands into it, then touched his blessed face, on account of the excessive heat that he felt: then he said, 'O Lord assist me in my hard condition' (i. e. the last moments of dying).

359.

Whoever loveth to meet God, God loveth to meet him.

360.

The rights of women are sacred. See

that women are maintained in the rights attributed to them.

361.

Death is a favour to a Muslim.

362.

One of the family of the Messenger of God died, and the women assembled, crying over the corpse, and Omar stood up to prevent them from crying, and drive them away: but Lord Muhammad said, 'Let them alone, O Omar, because eyes are shedders of tears; and the heart is stricken with calamity and sorrowful; and the time of misfortune near and fresh; and the crying of the women is without wailing.' (cf. p. 14).

363.

Verily a man used to come before the Rasûl, bringing his son with him; and the Rasûl said to him, 'Dost thou love this boy?' And the man said, 'O

Rasūl of God! may God love thee as I love this son!' Then the Rasūl did not see the boy with his father for some time; and he said, 'What has become of that man's son?' They said, 'O Rasūl! he is dead.' And the Rasūl said to the man, 'Dost thou not like this, that thou wilt find no door of Paradise but thy son will be there awaiting thee, in order to conduct thee into Paradise?' And another man said, 'O Rasūl! Is this joyful news particularly for this man, or for the whole of us?' Lord Muhammad said, 'For all of you.'

364.

The Rasūl visited his mother's grave, and wept, and caused those standing around him to weep also; that is, he wept to such a degree as to move the rest.

365.

The Rasūl passed by graves in Medinah, and turned his face toward them, and said, 'Peace to you, O people of the graves! May God forgive us and you: You have passed on before us, and we are following you!'

366.

A virtuous wife is a man's best treasure.

367.

Verily it is better for any of you to take your rope and bring a bundle of wood upon your back and sell it, in which case God guardeth your honour, than to beg of people, whether they give or not; if they do not give, your reputation suffereth, and you return disappointed; and if they give, it is worse than that; for it layeth you under obligation.

368.

Monopoly is unlawful in Islām.

369.

God is gentle and loveth gentleness.

370.

The Rasūl said, (when he was in the pulpit, and was mentioning the rewards of alms, and the advantages of avoiding begging), 'The upper hand is better than the lower;' and he said, 'The upper hand is the giver of alms, and the lower is the beggar.'

371.

Whoever hath food for a day and night, it is prohibited him to beg.

372.

Verily it is not right for the rich to ask, nor for a strong, robust, person; but it is allowable for an indigent, very needy person.

373.

I said to the Rasūl, 'May I beg

from people, O Rasūl, when necessitous?' Lord Muhammad said, 'No, do not beg; but if thou art absolutely compelled, then beg from the virtuous.'

374.

Paradise is not for him who reproacheth others with obligation after giving.

375.

Two qualities are not combined in any Muslim, one avarice, the other a bad disposition.

376.

Every good act, in which is approaching to the court of God, is charity [1].

377.

If I were disposed to trouble my

---

1 That is, the term charity is not confined, to the bestowing of worldly goods; but every act, such as kind words and behaviour, which tends to promote the happiness of others, comes under that denomination.

disciples, verily I would order them to clean their teeth at the time of every prayer[1].

378.

Lord Muhammad said, 'It is indispensable for every Muslim to give alms.' The companions said, 'But if he hath not any thing to give?' He said, 'If he hath nothing, he must do a work with his hand, by which to obtain something, and benefit himself; and give alms with the remainder.' They said, 'If he is not able to do that work, to benefit himself and give alms to others? The Rasūl said, 'Then assist the needy and oppressed.' They said, 'If he is not able to assist the oppressed?' He said, 'Then exhort people to do good.' 'And if he does not?' He said, 'Then let him withhold himself from doing harm

1 A Muslim prays five times a day, and each prayer is preceded by the prescribed ablution.

to people; for verily that is as alms and charity for him.'

379.

Doing justice between two people is charity; and assisting a man upon his beast, and lifting his baggage, is charity; and pure words in which be rewards; and answering a questioner with mildness, is charity; and removing that which is an inconvenience to man, such as thorns and stones, is charity.

380.

There is no Muslim who planteth a tree, or soweth a field, and man, birds or beasts eat from them, but it is charity for him.

381.

An adulteress was forgiven who passed by a dog at a well; and when the dog was holding out his tongue from thirst, which was near killing him the woman drew off her boot, and tied it to the end of her garment, and drew water for the dog, and gave him to drink; and she was forgiven for that act.

382.

Lord Muhammad said, 'A woman was punished for a cat, which she tied, till it died with hunger; and that woman gave the cat nothing to eat, nor did she set it at liberty, so that it might have eaten the reptiles of the ground.'

383.

'Verily are there rewards for our doing good to quadrupeds, and giving them water to drink?' Lord Muhammad said, 'There are rewards for benefiting every animal having a moist liver' (e. i. every one alive). [1]

---

1 In the Kur'ān, animal life stands on the same footing as human life in the sight of God. 'There is no beast on earth', says the Kur'ān, 'nor bird which flieth with its wings, but the same is a people like unto you (mankind) — unto the Lord shall they return.'

384.

Every good act is charity; and verily it is of the number of good acts to meet your brother with an open countenance, and to pour water from your own bag into his vessel.

385.

Your smiling in your brother's face is charity; and your exhorting mankind to virtuous deeds is charity; and your prohibiting the forbidden, is charity; and your shewing men the road, in the land in which they lose it, is charity for you; and your assisting the blind, is charity for you.

386.

Whoever bringeth the dead land to life; that is, cultivateth waste land, for him is reward therein.

387.

I came to Medinah, and saw a man

whose counsels men obeyed, and he never said anything but they obeyed him. I said, 'Who is this man?' They said, 'This is the Rasûl of God'. Then I went to him and said, 'Give me advice'. Lord Muhammad said, 'Abuse nobody.' And I never did abuse anybody after that, neither freeman nor slave, nor camel nor goat. And he added, 'And if a man abuse thee, and lay open a vice which he knoweth in thee; then do not disclose one which thou knowest in him.'

388.

Verily, the people of the Rasūl's house killed a goat, and the Rasūl said, 'What remaineth of it?' 'Ā'ishah said, 'Nothing but its shoulder; for they have sent the whole to the poor and neighbours, except a shoulder which remaineth.' The Rasūl said. 'The whole goat remaineth except its shoulder; that is, that remaineth which they have given away, and what remaineth in the house is frail.'

389.

The angels said, 'O God! Is there anything of thy creation harder than rocks?' God said, 'Yes; iron is harder than rocks, for it breaketh them.' The angels said, 'O Lord! Is there anything of thy creation harder than iron?' God said, 'Yes; fire is harder than iron, for it melteth it.' And the angels said, 'O defender! Is there anything of thy creation harder than fire?' God said, 'Yes; water overcometh fire: it killeth it and maketh it cold.' Then the angels said, 'O Lord! Is there anything of thy creation harder than water?' God said, 'Yes; wind overcometh water: it agitateth it and putteth it in motion.' They said, 'O our cherisher! Is there anything of thy creation harder than wind?' God said, 'Yes, the children of Adam, giving alms; that is, those who give with their right hands and conceal it from their left, overcome all.'

390.

The most excellent of alms is that of a man of small property, which he has earned by labour, from which he giveth as much as he is able.

391.

Giving alms to the poor hath the reward of one alms; but that given to kindred hath two rewards; one, the reward of alms, the other, the reward of helping relations.

392.

A man whilst fasting must abstain from all bad expressions, and not even resent an injury.

393.

A keeper of fast, who doth not abandon lying and detraction, God careth not about his leaving off eating and drinking; that is, God doth not accept his fasting.

394.

A man's first charity should be to his own family, if poor.

395.

God saith, 'I am near the hope of whoso putteth it in Me; and I am with him, and near him, when he remembereth Me.'

396.

God saith, 'Whoso doth one good act, for him are ten rewards; and I also give more to whomever I will; and whoso doth an ill, its retaliation is equal to it, or I forgive him; and whoso seeketh to approach Me one span, I seek to approach one cubit; and whoso seeketh to approach Me one cubit, I seek to approach him two fathoms; and whoso walketh towards Me, I run towards him; and who cometh before Me with the earth full of sins, and believeth solely in Me, him I come before with a front of forgiveness like that.'

397.

God saith, 'The person I hold as a beloved, I am his hearing by which he heareth, and I am his sight by which he seeth, and I am his hands by which he holdeth, and I am his feet by which he walketh.'

398.

God saith, "O Man! only follow thou My laws, and thou shalt become like unto Me, and then say, 'Be' and behold, It is." [1]

399.

'There is a polish for everything that taketh away rust; and the polish for the heart is the remembrance of God.'

---

1 i. e. If a person is in tune with the universe and in complete harmony with the laws of nature, then his will is in accord with the Divine will and whatever such a person willeth cometh to pass.

The companions said, 'Is not fighting with the infidels also like this?' Lord Muhammad said, 'No, although he fight until his sword be broken!'

400.

God is a unit, and liketh unity.

401.

We were with the Rasūl on a journey, and some men stood up repeating aloud, 'God is most great;' and the Rasūl said, 'O men! be easy on yourselves, and do not distress yourselves by raising your voices; verily you do not call to one deaf or absent, but verily to one who heareth and seeth; and He is with you; and He to whom you pray is nearer to you than the neck of your camel.' [1]

402.

Verily, my heart is veiled with

---

1 Cf. 'We are nearer him (man) than the vital vein.' — Kur'ān, *50.* 15.

melancholy and sadness for my followers; and verily I ask pardon of God one hundred times daily.

403.

Lord Muhammad said, 'I would not value having the whole wealth of the world in the place of this revelation, 'Say: (O Muhammad!) O My servants who have oppressed your own souls, despair not of the mercy of God [1].' A man said, 'What is the condition of him who hath associated others with God'? Lord Muhammad remained silent; after that he said, 'Know that him also God forgiveth; but on repentance.'

404.

A sincere repenter of faults is like him who hath committed none.

---

1 Kur'ān, *39*. 54. — Verily all sins doth God forgive; aye, Loving, Merciful, is He! And return ye to your Lord, and to Him resign yourselves, ere it is too late. (Addressed to the apostates from Islām).

405.

God saith, 'Verily My compassion overcometh My wrath'.

406.

Verily for God are one hundred lovingkindnesses; one of which He hath sent down amongst man, quadrupeds and every moving thing upon the face of earth: then by it they are kind to each other, and forgive one another; and by it the animals of the wilds are kind to their young; and God hath reserved ninety-nine lovingkindnesses, by which He will be gracious to His creatures on the last day.

407.

The Garden is nearer you than the thongs of your sandals; and the Fire likewise.

408.

The Rasūl said, 'Do you think this

woman will cast her own child into the fire?' We said, 'No'. Lord Muhammad said, 'Verily God is more compassionate on his creatures, than this woman on her own child.'

409.

A man came before the Rasûl with a carpet, and said, 'O Rasûl! I passed through a wood, and heard the voices of the young of birds; and I took and put them into my carpet; and their mother came fluttering round my head, and I uncovered the young, and the mother fell down upon them, then I wrapped them up in my carpet; and there are the young which I have.' Then the Rasūl said, 'Put them down.' And when he did so, their mother joined them: and Lord Muhammad said, 'Do you wonder at the affection of the mother towards her young? I swear by Him who hath sent me, verily God is more loving to his creatures than the mother to these young birds. Return them to the place from which ye took them, and let their mother be with them'.

410.

I saw Omar kiss the Black Stone, and say, 'Verily I know that thou art a stone; thou dost no good or harm in the world; and if it was not that I saw Lord Muhammad kiss thee, I would not kiss thee.' [1]

411.

I said to my mother, 'Describe Lord Muhammad to me.' She said, 'O my little son! had you seen him, you would say that you had seen a rising sun.'

412.

I never saw any thing more beautiful

1 He said this in order that people might not worship it.

than Lord Muhammad: you might say the sun was moving in his face.'

413.

I served Lord Muhammad ten years, and he never said 'Uff', [1] to me; and never said, 'Why did you do so?' and never said, 'Why did you not do so?'

414.

The Rasūl was the handsomest of men, and the most liberal, and the most brave.

415.

Lord Muhammad was more modest than a virgin behind her curtain.

416.

The other messengers of God had their miracles, mine is the Kur'ān and will remain forever.

---

1 An exclamation expressive of displeasure.

417.

There was a slave-girl of Medinah who used to take Lord Muhammad by the hand, and lead him wherever she pleased, and represent her circumstances to him.

418.

What did Lord Muhammad do within doors? 'He used to serve his family, such as milking goats, mending shoes and stitching; and when prayer-times came, he would go out to perform them.'

419.

Lord Muhammad never struck any one, or any thing with his own hand; and on his own account never felt revenge; save when people did things unlawful, then he would punish.

420.

God saith, 'I was a hidden treasure. I would fain be known. So I created Man.'

421.

Lord Muhammad used to wait upon himself.

422.

Lord Muhammad said, 'My cherisher hath ordered me nine things: (1) To reverence Him, externally and internally; (2) to speak true, and with propriety, in prosperity and adversity; (3) moderation in affluence and poverty; (4) to benefit my relations and kindred, who do not benefit me; (5) to give alms to him who refuseth me; (6) to forgive him who injureth me; (7) that my silence should be in attaining a knowledge of God; (8) that when I speak, I should mention Him; (9) that when I look on God's creatures, it should be as an example for them: and God hath ordered me to direct in that which is lawful.

423.

The taker of usury and the giver of

it, and the writer of its papers and the witness to it, are equal in crime.

424.

The holder of a monopoly is a sinner and offender.

425.

The bringers of grain to the city to sell at a cheap rate gain immense advantage by it, and whoso keepeth back grain in order to sell at a high rate is cursed.

426.

Whoso desireth that God should redeem him from the sorrows and travail of the last day, must delay in calling on poor debtors, or forgive the debt in part or whole.

427.

A martyr shall be pardoned every fault but debt.

428.

Whoso hath a thing wherewith to discharge a debt, and refuseth to do it, it is right to dishonour and punish him.

429.

Give the labourer his wage before his perspiration be dry.

430.

Do not prevent your women from coming to the mosque; but their homes are better for them.

431.

What was in the beginning? Lord Muhammad said, 'God was, and nothing was with Him: and He created His imperial throne upon water, and everything was in the tablet of His memory.'

432.

When were you confirmed a messenger? 'I was when Adam was yet between soul and body.'

'I was near God and Adam was still in his own clay.'

433.

Deal gently with the people, and be not harsh; cheer them and contemn them not. And ye will meet with many 'people of the book' who will question thee, what is the key to heaven? Reply to them (the key to heaven is) *to testify to the truth of God, and to do good work.*

434.

Do you love your Creator? love your fellow-beings first.

435.

To listen to the words of the learned, and to instil into others the lessons of science, is better than religious exercises.

436.

The ink of the scholar is more holy than the blood of the martyr.

437.

He who leaveth home in search of knowledge, walketh in the path of God.

438.

One hour's meditation on the work of the Creator is better than seventy years of prayer.

439.

Every moral agent is furthered to his own conduct.

440.

God is pure and loveth purity and cleanliness.

441.

God hath treasuries aneath the Throne, the keys whereof are the tongues of poets.

442.

The acquisition of knowledge is a duty incumbent on every Muslim, male and female.

443.

Acquire knowledge. It enableth its

possessor to distinguish right from wrong; it lighteth the way to Heaven; it is our friend in the desert, our society in solitude, our companion when friendless; it guideth us to happiness; it sustaineth us in misery; it is an ornament amongst friends, and an armour against enemies [1].

444.

With knowledge man riseth to the heights of goodness and to a noble position, associateth with sovereigns in this world, and attaineth to the perfection of happiness in the next.

445.

O Lord, grant to me the love of Thee; grant that I love those that love Thee; grant that I may do the deeds that win Thy love; make Thy love dearer to me than self, family or than wealth.

---

1 The present day Muslims should bear in mind this remarkable utterance of the 'Illiterate Prophet'.

446.

O Lord! I make my complaint unto Thee, out of my feebleness, and the vanity of my wishes. I am insignificant in the sight of men, O Thou most merciful! Lord of the weak! Thou art my Lord! Forsake me not. Leave me not a prey to strangers, nor to mine enemies. If Thou art not offended, I am safe. I seek refuge in the light of Thy countenance, by which all darkness is dispelled, and peace cometh in the Here and the Hereafter. Solve Thou my difficulties as it pleaseth Thee. There is no power, no strength, save in Thee [1].

---

1 This prayer was uttered by Lord Muhammad in a moment of deep distress. The idolaters of Ṭā'if had driven him out of the city. The rabble and the slaves, followed, hooting and pelting him with stones until the evening. Wounded and bleeding, footsore and weary, he betook himself to prayer.

447.

Keep fast and eat also, stay awake at night and sleep also, for verily there is a duty on you to your body, not to labour overmuch, so that ye may not get ill and destroy yourselves; and verily there is a duty on you to your eyes, ye must sometimes sleep and give them rest; and verily there is a duty on you to your wife, and to your visitors and guests that come to see you; ye must talk to them; and nobody hath kept fast who fasted always; the fast of three days in every month is equal to constant fasting: then keep three days' fast in every month.

448.

It was said to the Rasūl, 'O messenger of God! Curse the infidels.' Lord Muhammad said, 'I am not sent for this; nor was I sent but as a mercy to mankind.'

449.

Usāmah bin Zaid, relates from the Rasūl, in the word of God, 'After that I gave a book of laws, to those that were selected from My servants; then some of these injure their own souls, some of them observe a medium in their actions, and some of them are swift in goodness.' Lord Muhammad said, '*All of them are in Paradise, agreeable to their difference in eminence and degree.*'

450.

What is Paradise? Lord Muhammad said, 'It is what the eye hath not seen, nor the ear heard, nor ever flashed across the mind of man.'

451.

Verily God will send to this people, at the beginning of each age, him who shall renew its religion.[1]

---

[1] *A new century has begun. Where is the expected Restorer?*

APPENDIX.

al-KUR'ĀN.

Sūrah 2.

These are they who have bartered Right
for Wrong —
A bootless bargain, guideless left to
stray.
Their likeness is the likeness of one who
Kindles a fire, and when it lights up all
Around him all at once their visual
light
God takes away and leaves them in the
dark,
In utter darkness seeing naught at all!—
Deaf, dumb, blind, irrecoverably lost.
Or like a sweeping storm-cloud from
the sky
With darkness, thunder, and with light-
ning fraught —

With dread of death struck they stop their ears
With fingers and shut out the thunder's roar,
The while God hems in all the faithless folks —
The lightning well-nigh snatcheth off their sights;
Whene'er it gleameth, lo! they walk therein,
When darkness cometh on they halt and stop!
Had God but willed their hearing and their sight
Would He take off: Almighty God is He.

v. 59 It matters not whate'er ye name yourselves —
Believing Muslims, Jews or Nazarenes
Or Sâbians — whoe'er believe in God,
The last e'erlasting Day, and *act aright*,
Their meed is with their Lord; no fear nor care

Shall come upon them, nor the touch of woe.

God brings the dead to life and shows His signs
To you, that haply ye may understand.
Yet hard became your hearts e'en after that,
Till they were as stones or harder still.
For of stones be some from which streams
Burst forth, and of them there be some that burst
Asunder and the water issues out,
And of them there be some that falleth down
For fear and majesty and awe of God.
And God is careless ne'er of what ye do.

Sūrah 94.

In God's name, the Loving, the Merciful.

Did We not broaden thy breast?
And lifted off thee thy load that pressed

Heavily, and sorely thy back distressed?
And heaved thy name high above the rest?
Then verily with woe there is weal!
Verily with woe there is weal!
So when thou hast admonished and thy preaching finished
Draw nigh unto Me, nigh unto thy Lord.

INDEX.

The numbers refer to the Sayings.

A.

B.

C.

D.

E.

F.

G.

H.

I.

J.

N.

O.

P.

R.

S.

T.

U.

V.

W.

CPSIA information can be obtained at www.ICGtesting.com
Printed in the USA
LVOW06s0244281215

468056LV00021B/473/P